Michael Bond's
BOOK OF
BEARS

Michael O'Mara Books Limited

This book is dedicated to 'LIBEARTY' – The World Campaign For Bears. World Society for the Protection of Animals, 10 Lawn Lane, London SW8 1UD. Tel: 0171 793 0540

First published in 1992 by
Michael O'Mara Books Ltd
9 Lion Yard
Tremadoc Road
London SW4 7NQ

This edition published in 1995

Michael Bond's Book of Bears Copyright © 1992 by Michael O'Mara Books Ltd

A CIP catalogue record for this book is available from the British Library

ISBN 1-85479-111-7

Designed by Pinpoint Design
Typeset by DP Photosetting, Aylesbury, Bucks

Printed in Hong Kong by Midas Printing Co.

Contents

Acknowledgments

The publishers are grateful to the following for permission to reproduce copyright material.

Michael Bond's introduction to his Book of Bears and his introduction to the stories are © Michael Bond 1992. The story 'Paddington takes over' is © Michael and Karen Bond 1992.
'The half-price bear' is reproduced by permission of the author Frances Lindsay. First published 1986 by Hodder and Stoughton.
'How Bruiny came to live next door' by Enid Blyton is © Darrell Waters Limited 1944 and was first published in *Tales of Toyland* by Newnes 1944.
'Bozzy finds a friend' is reproduced by permission of the author Graham J Brooks, and John Martin and Artists Limited © 1992.
'Teddy Robinson keeps house' by Joan G Robinson from *Teddy Robinson's Second Omnibus* is reproduced by permission of Harrap Publishing Group.
'Which bear's best?' by Anne Forsyth is reproduced by permission of the author © 1992.
'What can I do today?' by Elizabeth Brook is reproduced by permission of the author © 1992.
'Little Bear's wish' by Else Holmelund Minarik is reproduced from *Little Bear* by permission of Laurence Pollinger Limited and HarperCollins Publishers © 1957 by Else Homelund Minarik.
'The treasure hunt' is reproduced by permission of the author Lesley Smith, and John Martin and Artists Limited © 1992.
'The bear who went to sea' by Kate Marshall is reproduced by permission of the author © 1992.
'Grizzwold' by Syd Hoff is reproduced by permission of World's Work Limited © Syd Hoff 1963.
'Bluff and Bran and the tree house' by Meg Rutherford is reproduced by permission of Andre Deutsch Limited © Meg Rutherford 1986
'Teddy's story' by Rose Impey and Sue Porter is reproduced by permission of William Heinemann Limited, text © Rose Impey 1988.
'The bears of the air' by Arnold Lobel is reproduced by permission of World's Work Limited © Arnold Lobel 1965.

Illustration Acknowledgments

The publishers are grateful to the following for permission to reproduce copyright material.

Ray Mutimer for illustrations to 'Paddington takes over' by Michael Bond © Paddington & Co.
Bridget Dowty for illustrations to 'The half-price bear' by Frances Lindsay.
Darrell Waters Limited for illustrations to 'How Bruiny came to live next door' by Enid Blyton © 1944.
Cathie Shuttleworth and John Martin and Artists Limited © 1992 for illustrations to 'Bozzy finds a friend' by Graham Brooks.
Joan G. Robinson and Harrap Publishing Group for illustrations to 'Teddy Robinson keeps house'.
Jan Brychta for illustrations to 'Which bear's best?' by Anne Forsyth.
Laurence Pollinger Limited and Harper Collins Publishers for illustrations to 'Little Bear's wish' by Maurice Sendak © 1957.
Lesley Smith and John Martin and Artists Limited for illustrations to 'The treasure hunt' by Lesley Smith © 1992.
Patrick Lowry and Michael Woodward Licensing for 'What can I do today' by Elizabeth Brook © 1992.
Syd Hoff for illustrations to 'Grizzwold'.
Meg Rutherford and Andre Deutsch for illustrations to 'Bluff and Bran and the tree house'.
Sue Porter for illustrations to 'Teddy's story' by Rose Impey and Sue Porter © 1988.
Arnold Lobel for illustrations to 'The bears of the air' © 1965.

The publishers would like to thank the Early Children's Book Collection, Wandsworth Libraries, London for their help.

Introduction

Bears have been objects of worship and veneration from time immemorial.

It is easy to see why early man looked up to such splendidly noble and powerful creatures – they had to! Heading down into the valley from its mountain lair in search of food after a long winter sleep, your average member of the family *Ursidae* must have been an awesome sight as it reared up on its two hind legs in order to take stock of the surrounding countryside.

It's a variation on that old joke – 'What do you call an escaped gorilla?' Answer: 'Sir!'

There must have been a certain symbolism, too, in the way that the appearance of the first bear heralded the coming of spring; 'bear festivals' still form part of springtime celebrations in various parts of the world.

It is a little harder to say quite why the humble Teddy is so universally revered. Perhaps it is because, unlike his real life counterpart, he is totally undemanding.

Dolls are forever wondering what to wear next and have things called 'outfits' for special occasions. They worry about the latest fashions and on the whole are very unbending creatures; stiff and starchy. You'd certainly think twice before telling a doll anything confidential – as like as not it would be passed on to the very first person who came along.

Bears are quite the opposite. There they sit, or stand or lie, thinking their thoughts; content with their lot.

Not that there is any need to feel sorry for them. On the whole they don't do too badly in their own quiet way. True, the less exalted may have to make do with the occasional picnic or 'midnight feast', but if some of the letters I receive are anything to go by, others lead lives of positively sybaritic luxury. They travel around the world with their owners, staying at first class hotels; they sit at table – no doubt supping the best of food and wine; some carry their own passport; others laboriously type 'thank you' letters on their own headed note-paper ('From the desk of E. Bear, Esq.' is not uncommon).

For many years I received regular telephone calls from one Oliver Q. Dodger – a contender if ever there was one for the list of ten best-dressed bears in the world; sweater from Paris, trousers from Madrid, gold bangle from Tiffany's. The calls eventually stopped, possibly because his owner couldn't afford the bills, which must have been quite considerable, or else Mr Dodger himself began to find the conversation was becoming a bit one-sided. Bears are sensitive to these things.

They are born with a wisdom beyond their years and, unlike dolls, you can tell them your innermost secrets knowing they won't divulge them to another soul, or be in the slightest bit censorious. It's hard to tell when a bear is raising its eyebrows anyway.

Perhaps this is part of their secret. In a world where somehow things are never quite what they used to be, it is comforting to have a friend who is not only loyal and uncritical, but at the same time remains so resolutely resistant to change. No matter what, your Teddy will stay exactly the same, steadfast and true, a symbol of constancy, your devoted slave through thick and thin for the whole of your life.

No home should be without one.

Not – as you will see from some of the following stories – that they are always GOOD. That would be too boring for words, and bears are many things, but they are never, ever boring.

Michael Bond

The half-price bear

FRANCES LINDSAY

> *Bears have a strong sense of right and wrong and their own particular way of putting matters to rights without blatantly resorting to telling tales.*
>
> MICHAEL BOND

Toby knew he was looking at a Very Special Bear the moment he saw it. It was sitting on the top shelf in Mr Totty's Toy Shop and had a large notice around its neck. Toby read aloud, 'HALF . . . PRICE . . . SHOP . . . SHOP . . .' He pointed to the last word. 'I'll sound it out. Ss . . . oil . . . ed . . . Soiled!'

'Well done,' said Mr Totty.

'What does it mean?' Toby asked.

'Half price means what it says . . .'

'I know that but what does the next bit mean?'

'It means that the bear has been in the shop rather a long time so I'm selling it cheap.' Mr Totty gave the bear a long, hard look and whispered, 'I've never known a bear like it. Never stays where I put it and no sooner have I tied its ribbon into a nice big bow than it comes undone.'

'Perhaps you don't tie the bow tightly enough. Perhaps you forget where you put the bear.'

Mr Totty looked annoyed. 'I never forget anything,' he said and went off to serve another customer.

Toby heard a chuckle and, looking up, he saw the bear

9

was laughing. Then it winked at Toby and undid its bow!
Toby could hardly believe his eyes. He knew bears who
squeaked when their tummies were pressed but he had
never seen a bear that laughed and winked and undid its
bow.

He looked at the police car on the counter – he had
meant to buy it with his birthday money. Then he looked
again at the bear. Toby's Mum came into the shop.

'We'll miss the bus if you don't hurry, Toby. Have you
bought the car you wanted?'

'I'm going to buy that bear instead.'

'But you've got a bear.'

'That's a teddy bear. This is . . .'

'A koala,' Mr Totty said quickly. 'A very nice bear
indeed. Koalas come from Australia; they're not really
bears like teddy bears but they're just as nice.'

'Well, I think he's a bear. He's an extra special kind of
bear.'

'Toby's a bit old for a bear, isn't he?' Mum asked.

Mr Totty looked hurt. 'You are never too old for a bear,
madam,' he said. He took the koala off the shelf, brushed it
and put it into a brown paper bag. Toby gave his birthday
money to Mr Totty and took the bear out of the bag. 'He
doesn't like being wrapped up,' he said.

'You'll have to give him a nice Australian name,' said
Mr Totty.

'Henry's a nice name for a bear,' said Mum.

'I'll call him Bim.'

'Bim?' said Mum.

'Bim?' said Mr Totty.

'His name is Bim,' said Toby firmly.

Going home on the bus the koala whispered, 'I'm glad you chose me.' Toby stared in surprise. 'You can talk!' he gasped.

'Ssh! It's a secret . . . I'm magic!'

Toby was excited and held Bim closer. 'What a nice bear,' said the lady in the seat behind Toby. She bent forward and the feather in her hat tickled the back of Bim's neck.

'He . . . He . . . He . . .' he chortled.

'Bless my soul!' she said. 'Did you hear that? The bear's laughing. I've never heard a bear laugh before. They've given him a laugh instead of a squeak in his middle – how clever! You must tell me where you bought him, little boy. I'd like to get one for my grandson.'

Toby didn't answer and his Mum said quickly,' He came from Mr Totty's toy shop.'

'Thank you. I'll remember that,' said the lady.

When it was time to get off the bus, Bim pulled off his bow, threw it under the seat and winked at the lady with the feather in her hat. 'Did you see that? He's real,' she gasped and her eyes closed.

'Quick, she's fainted!' shouted an old man.

At once the conductor took off his hat and fanned her with it. 'Don't do that!' she shouted angrily and hit him with her shopping bag.

'I was only trying to help,' said the conductor.

Toby's sisters were waiting at the bus stop. 'Did you get the police car?' they asked.

'I bought Bim instead.'

'He's nice,' said Jemma and shook Bim's paw.

'Better than a silly old police car,' said Beth.

Toby's Dad came along. 'Did you get the police car, Toby?'

'I bought Bim instead.'

'He's much better than a police car but he should have a smart bow tie. I'll give him the one with the big red spots that Aunt Maud sent me.' He looked at Mum and laughed.

'Thank you, Dad,' said Toby.

That night when everyone was asleep, Bim went into the bathroom because all his best ideas came when he was cleaning his teeth. The toothpaste tasted of peppermint toffee, Bim's favourite sweets – he often wished sausages tasted the same. At once he had a bright idea. He would go exploring.

He slid down the bannisters which was great fun, said 'Hello' to Bill the budgie, sat in the cat's basket and climbed on top of the grandfather clock. He looked at the pictures on the wall, opened cupboards, jars and tins and had a paddle in the sink in the kitchen. Then he felt tired and he knew it was time for bed. He tried to slide *up* the bannisters but he found it was harder than sliding down so he climbed the stairs instead and was soon snuggling down next to Toby.

Bim was fast asleep when Toby went to play football next morning. He woke when Toby's Mum came into the room. 'Now's my chance to get rid of all Toby's rubbish,' she said.

'There's no rubbish here,' said Bim.

Toby's Mum didn't answer. 'It's always the same,' thought Bim. 'Grown-ups never hear what I say.'

Toby's Mum took a big piece of seaweed off the wall and threw it on the floor. 'What cheek!' Bim cried.

Then she tipped a pile of yoghurt pots, plastic bottles, fir cones, shells and matchboxes on top. 'That's not rubbish! They're Special Things To Keep,' Bim shouted.

Toby's Mum took no notice but went on adding to the pile on the floor: old comics, an odd slipper, a pair of torn water wings, a broken bat, a pair of socks and a cardboard box full of odds and ends. She wrinkled her nose. 'There's a nasty smell in here,' she said. 'It's not me,' said Bim loudly.

Toby's Mum looked under the bed and pulled out a dead crab. 'Pooh!' she cried.

'H'm. It does smell a bit nasty,' said Bim, 'But it'll be all right if it's washed with scented soap.'

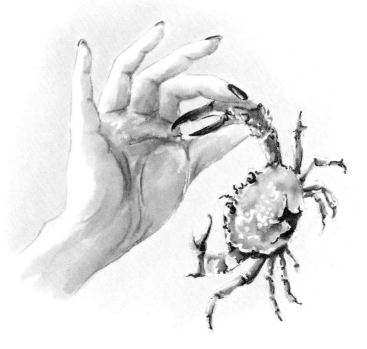

Toby's Mum put everything into a black sack. She took it downstairs and put it in the dustbin. Bim watched her from the window and when she went shopping he hurried downstairs and took everything out of the dustbin again. He carried the treasures back to Toby's room, except for the dead crab which smelt worse than ever. When Toby came home, Bim told him what he had done. Toby thanked him and said Bim had saved all his treasures.

'I'm sorry about the crab.'

'It doesn't matter. I found a mouse in the garden. I'll go and fetch it,' said Toby.

Next day Toby told Bim that Cousin James was coming to tea. 'He's very rough so I'm going to hide you under the bed where he won't see you.'

Bim didn't want to hide under the bed with the dead mouse and all the other treasures, so as soon as Toby had gone downstairs he climbed on to the windowsill and hid behind the curtain.

He pressed his nose against the glass and watched the children playing in the garden. He wished he was with them. Then a small boy with spiky red hair rushed into the garden, pushed Beth off her bike and tipped the dolls out of their pram.

'Silly old Beth! Silly old dolls!' he shouted and ran indoors.

Bim heard him creeping upstairs and saw him come into the room, take Toby's watch and stuff it in his pocket. In the girls' room he took something off the chest and put it in his other pocket. Then he went downstairs.

Toby was angry when Bim told him what he had seen.

'I know,' Bim said. 'Tell James you can walk faster on your hands than he can and ask your Mum and James's Mum to come and watch.'

Toby did as Bim said. James cried, 'No you can't! I bet I can walk much faster on my hands than you.' They all watched him go across the lawn and saw Toby's watch and Jemma's locket fall out of his pocket! James's Mum took him home in disgrace.

'You are the cleverest, most magical toy koala bear in the world,' said Toby.

Bim laughed. 'I know I am,' he said . . .

The three bears

TRADITIONAL

No book of bear stories would be complete without the story of Goldilocks and the Three Bears. Maddeningly repetitive and predictable – one is dying for Goldilocks to get on with it before the bears arrive back – and yet at the same time it would be a brave reader who dared to skip so much as a single word.

MICHAEL BOND

Once upon a time there were Three Bears who lived together in a house in a wood. One was a Small Wee Bear, and one was a Middle-sized Bear, and the other was a Great Huge Bear.

They each had a bowl for their porridge. There was a little bowl for the Small Wee Bear, and a middle-sized bowl for the Middle Bear, and a great bowl for the Great Huge Bear. And they had three chairs and three beds, little ones for the Small Wee Bear, middle-sized ones for the Middle Bear, and great big ones for the Great Huge Bear.

One day before breakfast, while they were waiting for their porridge to cool, they took a walk in the woods. And while they were away, young Goldilocks came to the house. First she looked in the window, then she peeped through the keyhole, and seeing nobody was at home she lifted the

The 3 Bears take a Morning Walk :

R Andre

latch. She went in and saw the bowls of porridge steaming on the table.

Now, if Goldilocks had been a good girl, she would have waited for the Bears to come home, and perhaps they would have asked her to breakfast. For they were good Bears – a little rough as many Bears are – but kind and friendly. But Goldilocks was a naughty girl, and she began to help herself.

So first she tasted the porridge of the Great Huge Bear, and that was too hot. She didn't like that. Then she tasted the porridge of the Middle Bear, and that was too cold. She didn't like that. And then she tasted the porridge of the Small Wee Bear, and that was just right. So she ate it all up.

Then Goldilocks sat down in the chair of the Great Huge Bear, and that was too hard. Then she sat in the chair of the Middle Bear, and that was too soft. And then she sat in the chair of the Small Wee Bear, and that was just right. So she sat there until the bottom came out of the chair and she went plump upon the ground. And then Goldilocks said a wicked word.

Then Goldilocks went upstairs into the bedroom. First she lay on the bed of the Great Huge Bear, but that was too high. Then she lay on the bed of the Middle Bear, but that was too low. And then she lay on the bed of the Small Wee Bear, and that was just right. So she pulled the bed-clothes up to her chin, and went fast asleep.

After a while, the Three Bears came home, as they expected the porridge to be cool by now. But when they looked at the table, they saw a spoon standing in each bowl of porridge.

:Somebody's Breakfast:

'SOMEBODY HAS BEEN AT MY PORRIDGE!'
said the Great Huge Bear in his loud, gruff voice.

And the Middle Bear saw the spoon in his bowl.

'Somebody has been at my porridge!'
said the Middle Bear in his middle-sized voice.

Then the Small Wee Bear saw the spoon in his bowl, and all his porridge was gone.

'Somebody has been at my porridge, and has eaten it all up!'
said the Small Wee Bear in his little, sharp voice.

When they found that their breakfast was disturbed, the Three Bears began to look around the house. The Great Huge Bear noticed that the cushion was not straight in his big, hard chair.

'SOMEBODY HAS BEEN SITTING IN MY CHAIR!'
said the Great Huge Bear in his loud, gruff voice.

And the Middle Bear saw a dent in the soft cushion of his chair.

'Somebody has been sitting in my chair!'
said the Middle Bear in his middle-sized voice.

And you know what Goldilocks had done to the third chair.

'Somebody has been sitting in my chair, and has broken the bottom out of it!'
said the Small Wee Bear in his little, sharp voice.

Then the Three Bears went upstairs to look in the bedroom. The Great Huge Bear saw the pillow out of place on his bed.

'SOMEBODY HAS BEEN LYING IN MY BED!'
said the Great Huge Bear in his loud, gruff voice.

And the Middle Bear saw that his bedspread was out of place.

'Somebody has been lying in my bed!' said the Middle Bear in his middle-sized voice.

And when the Small Wee Bear looked at his bed, he saw a head of golden hair lying on his pillow, and that was definitely out of place.

'Somebody has been lying in my bed – and here she is!' said the Small Wee Bear in his little, sharp voice.

In her sleep, Goldilocks heard the loud, gruff voice of the Great Huge Bear. But it seemed like the roar of the wind, or the rumble of thunder. And she heard the middle-sized voice of the Middle Bear. But it seemed like someone speaking in a dream. But when she heard the little, sharp voice of the Small Wee Bear, it was so sharp and shrill that she woke up at once.

Up she jumped. And when she saw the Three Bears on one side of the bed, looking very cross and bothered, she tumbled out of the other side and ran to the window. Now the Three Bears

Saved :

were good, tidy, healthy Bears, and they always opened their window in the morning. So Goldilocks leaped out of the window.

Perhaps she broke her neck in the fall. Or perhaps she ran into the wood and was lost. Or perhaps a policeman found her and took her away to the police station.

But the Three Bears never saw anything more of her.

Which bear's best?

ANNE FORSYTH

> *Being first isn't always the most*
> *important thing in life; it's*
> *where you end up that matters*
> *most.*
>
> MICHAEL BOND

'Class number 65 – a teddy bear,'
said Gran. 'If I start now, I could
make a teddy bear in time for the
show. Next time I go to town, I'll buy a pattern – that's
what I'll do. Then I'll make a bear.'

It was going to be the biggest, best farm show ever.
Every year people came from miles away to see the prize
cattle and horses and sheep. There was a dog show too,
and displays of tractors, and very old cars. You could buy
icecream and hot dogs and juice, and listen to the bands.
And in one of the biggest tents, was a display of knitting
and sewing, and jams and jellies, and baking – with scones
and sponge cakes as light as a feather. It was always very
hard for the judges to decide which was best.

Gran went to town and bought a pattern to make a
teddy bear. She used furry material for the bear's head and
brown felt for the pads on his paws. She gave him bright
twinkling eyes and stitched on his smile. When she had
finished, she looked at him. He was round and cheerful

with a brown snub nose. But –

'That bear,' said Uncle Joe. 'He looks very fine, but somehow he looks –'

'A bit naughty,' said Cousin Bill.

Gran looked again at the bear. Perhaps they were right. She had given him a spotted bow tie that was a little crooked. His ears flopped and somehow his eyes had a wicked sort of twinkle.

'If I saw that bear in a shop,' said Uncle Joe, 'I'd say he was up to mischief.'

'Well,' said Gran, 'maybe he is.' She gave him a pat on the head. 'I'm going to call him Barney.' She had got quite fond of the bear. She packed him up carefully and took him along to the show.

There were lots of other bears in the competition. Large bears and small bears and furry bears and knitted woolly bears. There was a very little bear and one enormous bear with a shiny bow tie. There was a bear dressed as a sailor, wearing a blue and white cap. Another bear wore striped dungarees in all different colours, and there was even a footballer bear – he wore a red and white strip and had a football at his feet.

Right at the front was the most handsome bear of all. He was quite perfect from his smart knitted hat to his furry paws.

'Look at *him!*' People smiled when they saw Barney. Well, his ears flopped in a funny way and Gran had stitched on his smile as if he were laughing.

The tent was busy with people bringing all sorts of things for the competitions – sausage rolls and scones and iced cakes and pots of jam and lemon curd, and lots more besides.

At last the tent was closed for the night. Everything was ready. The cakes were all covered up so that they didn't get dusty, and someone had swept up the rubbish. Next day the judges would arrive early, and decide on the winners in each class.

'Ah,' yawned a small bear. 'It's been a long day.'

'Well, I wonder who's going to be first in our class,' said the very handsome bear. He didn't like to say, 'I bet it's me,' but everyone knew that was what he was thinking.

'See that one next to you,' whispered a large furry bear to the sailor bear. 'Doesn't he look – well, a little odd?'

He didn't say it very loudly because bears are kind animals and don't like to hurt people's feelings. But Barney heard. And he heard the sailor bear give a laugh, and try to pretend it was a cough.

Barney felt a bit ashamed. He knew he didn't look as smart as the other bears.

But just then there was a sound of buzzing. Buzz . . . buzzz . . . buzzzz . . .

A large bee hovered over the soft toys, and hummed over the bears and finally settled on the nose of the sailor bear next to Barney.

'Keep quite still,' said the footballer bear. 'It will go away.'

'No, it won't,' said Barney. 'You leave it to me.' And he took a swing at the bee with his paw. The bee buzzed off, and Barney hit the sailor bear by mistake and knocked off his blue and white cap.

'You did that on purpose.' The bear picked up his cap and jammed it on his head.

'No, I didn't.'

'Yes, you did.'

He raised his paws as if he was going to fight.

'So you want a fight?' said Barney.

'Stop it, both of you!' A policeman bear raised his truncheon and stepped between them. 'That's quite enough.'

Barney felt quite upset. After all, he had only been trying to help. He hadn't meant to hit the sailor bear.

He yawned. 'I think I'll go for a walk,' he said. 'Anyone coming with me?'

No one spoke. They pretended they didn't hear him. Who wanted to go for a walk with this odd, rather scruffy-looking bear?

So Barney clambered down from the bench. He slid down the leg and landed with a thump on the grass. He picked himself up, waved to the other bears – who took no notice – and set off.

Barney wandered round the tent. He passed the soft toys and the knitted jerseys and socks, and he came to the table with the meat pasties and sausage rolls. Mmm . . . he sniffed.

And then, all of a sudden, he heard a very strange sound. Pad, pad, pad. He stood very still.

There it was again. Pad, pad, pad. He quickly scampered behind the cloth that covered the table. It hung right down to the ground, so no one could see him. He peeped out, and there, pushing through the opening in the tent, was a

very large black dog, with a thick, shaggy coat.

The bears and the other toys watched from their bench.

'What sort of animal is that?'

'It's fierce,' said one of the bears.

'Very fierce,' said another.

The soft toys began to shake and shiver. A scarecrow waved his arms. A guardsman doll began to huff and bluster: and an upside down doll thought she might be safer the other way up.

'Here!' said one of the toys.

'That bear – the funny-looking one – he's out there!'

Barney watched from his hiding place.

The dog passed by the jams and jellies and the cakes – and he didn't even sniff at the scones. But when he came to the meat pasties, he raised his head. He put both paws up on the table, sniffed at the paper covering, and was just about to snap when –

'Grrrr . . .' There was a low, deep growl from under the table.

'Grrrr . . .' It was Barney, of

course, growling as loudly as he could.

The dog was so surprised that he turned and ran – out through the tent flap, out of the field, and straight back home. He wasn't going back to that tent, not for the best meat pasty in the world. What was under the table? He didn't want to wait to find out.

Barney came out of his hiding place, and made his way back to join the other bears.

'Well done!' they all squeaked.

'You were brave!' squeaked the upside down doll.

'Good show,' said the sailor bear.

'You'll have to help me,' said Barney, and all the bears reached down to lend him a paw, and haul him up.

When they'd pulled him up, they patted him on the back, and he smiled his lopsided smile. 'It was nothing,' he said.

Next day, when the judges came round, they knew right away who should be first.

Barney?

Oh, no, it was the very handsome bear right in the front. The sailor bear was second, and the footballer bear third.

When Gran came along to see the show that afternoon, she was surprised to notice that Barney's fur was all ruffled, and his bow tie even more crooked. 'You've been up to something,' she said to him.

'Oh, look at the bears!' Three small children were standing gazing at them. 'Aren't they beautiful?' said the little girl.

'I like that one best.' Her brother pointed to Barney.

Gran heard him. 'Would you like to have that bear?' she said. 'I made him. You can take him home at the end of the show.'

'Oh, no, really. You mustn't,' said the children's mother.

'My children are all grown up. Even my grandchildren are too big for bears,' said Gran. 'I'd like Barney to go to a really good home.'

'Look at him,' said one of the children. 'He's got lovely ears. And see – he's smiling at us.'

'He looks very bold and brave,' said the youngest. 'I bet he's brave.'

All the bears nodded and smiled and clapped their paws together.

But oddly enough – no one noticed!

Little Bear's wish

ELSE HOLMELUND MINARIK

Wishing doesn't always make it so, especially when
you wish for something as far away as the moon.
Sometimes, as Little Bear discovers, it's better if
you set your sights nearer home.

MICHAEL BOND

'Little Bear,' said Mother Bear.

'Yes, Mother,' said Little Bear.

'You are not asleep,' said Mother Bear.

'No, Mother,' said Little Bear.

'I can't sleep.'

'Why not?' said Mother Bear.

'I'm wishing,' said Little Bear.

'What are you wishing for?' said Mother Bear.

'I wish that I could sit on a cloud and fly all around,' said Little Bear.

'You can't have that wish, my Little Bear,' said Mother Bear.

'Then I wish that I could find a Viking boat,' said Little Bear.

'And the Vikings would say, "Come along, come along!

Here we go. Away! Away!" '

'You can't have that wish, my Little Bear,' said Mother Bear.

'Then I wish I could find a tunnel,' said Little Bear.

'Going all the way to China. I would go to China and come back with chopsticks for you.'

'You can't have that wish, my Little Bear,' said Mother
Bear.

'Then I wish I had a big red car,' said Little Bear.

'I would go fast, fast. I would come to a big castle. A

princess would come out and say, "Have some cake, Little
Bear," and I would have some.'

'You can't have that wish, my Little Bear,' said Mother
Bear.

'Then I wish,' said Little Bear, 'a Mother Bear would
come to me and say, "Would you like to hear a story?"'

'Well,' said Mother Bear, 'maybe you can have that wish.
That is just a little wish.'

'Thank you, Mother,' said Little Bear. 'That was what I really wanted all the time.'

'What kind of story would you like to hear?' said Mother Bear.

'Tell me about me,' said Little Bear. 'Tell me about
things I once did.'

'Well,' said Mother Bear, 'once you played in the snow,
and you wanted something to put on.'

'Oh, yes, that was fun,' said Little Bear. 'Tell me something more about me.'

'Well,' said Mother Bear, 'once you put on your space helmet and played going to the moon.'

'That was fun, too,' said Little Bear. 'Tell me more about me.'

'Well,' said Mother Bear, 'once you thought you had no Birthday Cake, so you made Birthday Soup.'

'Oh, that was fun,' said Little Bear. 'And then you came with the cake. You always make me happy.'

'And now,' said Mother Bear, 'you can make me happy, too.'

'How?' said Little Bear.

'You can go to sleep,' said Mother Bear.

'Well, then, I will,' said Little Bear. 'Good night, Mother dear.'

'Good night, Little Bear. Sleep well.'

Paddington takes over

MICHAEL AND KAREN BOND

Writing a Paddington story is a bit like making a cake. You put lots of different ingredients into a bowl and stir them all together. Then you put the mixture into the oven, close the door, and stand clear. When it's marmalade-making time you would be wise to stand very clear. Anything can happen, and usually does.

MICHAEL BOND

One morning Paddington arrived downstairs for breakfast at number thirty-two Windsor Gardens, only to find the dining-room was far from being its normal sunny self. In fact, glancing round the room as he took his place at the table, he decided everyone was looking extremely gloomy, which was most unusual.

Following normal practice, Mr Brown had been served first so that he could rush off to the office, but for once he seemed in no hurry to leave.

'I'll have another cup of tea, please, Mary,' he said, absentmindedly holding up an empty plate. 'I feel very thirsty this morning.'

'I'm not surprised,' said Mrs Brown. She exchanged glances with the others as she swopped his plate for a cup. 'If you will put salt on your cornflakes instead of sugar, you're bound to be thirsty. *And* you put sugar on your

48

bacon and eggs. I don't know what's come over you.'

'Oh, dear,' said Mr Brown. 'No wonder it was all crunchy. I'm sorry, Mary. My mind's on other things.' He tapped a large envelope in front of him. 'I'm having trouble with a take-over bid.'

'What's a take-over bid?' asked Jonathan.

'Quite simply,' said Mr Brown, 'it means that when one company wants to buy up another, it makes an offer. It's a bit like buying something in an auction. It happens practically every day in the City, but this time there's a snag because we can't deliver it.'

'Why don't you post it?' asked Judy.

Mr Brown shook his head. 'It has to be handed to the Chairman of the company in person and that's the problem. No-one ever gets to meet him. His name is Sir Granville Holmes-Bottomley and his office is right at the top of a skyscraper. They call him the Scarlet Pimpernel because no-one ever sees him come or go. The trouble is he ought to retire but he won't give up the reins. Anyway, today is the last possible day for making the bid, so it wouldn't get there in time.'

'How about if you landed on the roof from a helicopter?' suggested Jonathan. 'That would surprise him.'

'Perhaps not,' he added hastily, as he caught the look on Mr Brown's face.

The others fell silent while they considered the problem. Paddington was so lost in thought he put a large dollop of marmalade in his mug by mistake and when he stirred his cocoa it went all over the table cloth.

'It must be catching,' said Mrs Bird, the Browns'

housekeeper, as she mopped up the mess. 'The sooner it's all over and done with the happier I shall be. I don't know about take-over bids,' she added darkly, 'I shall be taking off if I have to put up with this sort of thing much longer!'

'I'll tell you something,' said Mr Brown. 'If this deal doesn't go through, bang goes our summer holiday. In fact, bang go a lot of people's holidays.' And with that, he rose to his feet, picked up his brief case and left for the office carrying Mrs Bird's sunshade instead of his rolled umbrella.

It wasn't until some time later, when Mrs Bird was clearing away the breakfast things that she noticed Mr Brown had forgotten his envelope. By that time Mrs

Brown had gone out and Jonathan and Judy were nowhere to be found. There was only Paddington left.

'Mercy me!' she cried. 'What *are* we going to do. I've got the gas man coming and I daren't trust it to a taxi driver. Mr Brown will never forgive me if it gets lost.'

Paddington jumped to his feet. 'I'll take it if you like, Mrs Bird,' he exclaimed. 'Bears are good at doing deliveries.'

The Browns' housekeeper gazed at Paddington dubiously. 'If you're visiting the City,' she said firmly, 'you can't go looking like that. You'd better have a quick bath first and get rid of your breakfast stains.'

Paddington began to wish he'd never suggested it. 'I'm glad I don't work in the City if it means having a bath every day,' he announced.

Nevertheless, he did as he was told, and by the time he came back downstairs again, apart from a few suds sticking to the back of his head, he was looking remarkably clean and tidy. There was also a thoughtful gleam in his eye. Paddington had often found that having a hot bath brought on ideas and today was no exception. Normally Mrs Bird would have been quick to recognise the signs, but luckily for her peace of mind she had other things to worry about.

She gave Paddington's duffle coat a quick going over with the vacuum cleaner and then pressed some money into his paw.

'I've asked the taxi driver to stop in the market on the way,' she said. 'If you take your shopping basket on wheels you can get some Seville oranges while they are still around. If things are as bad as Mr Brown says they are, I'd best be making a good supply of marmalade while the going's good. We don't want to run short during the long winter months.'

Paddington waved goodbye to Mrs Bird as he climbed into the waiting taxi and set off towards the Portobello Road. He was a well-known figure in the market so it wasn't long before he arrived back with his basket full to the brim with oranges.

'Where to now, guv'?' asked the driver, after he'd seen his fare safely inside the cab.

Paddington waited until they had turned a corner before replying. He didn't want anyone to overhear, and he wasn't the sort of bear who believed in taking chances. When he was sure they were safely on their way, he passed Mr Brown's envelope through a gap in the sliding window for the driver to see. 'I'd like to go to there, please,' he announced.

The driver gave a whistle as he took in the address. He glanced back over his shoulder with new respect.

'No wonder you've got your best bib and tucker on,' he said. 'I don't often get to take people to see Sir Granville.'

'I'm not sure that you will be now,' said Paddington unhappily. He stared out at some tall buildings looming up on either side of him. At the start of the journey, he had felt very optimistic, but the nearer he got to his destination the more he began to have second thoughts on the matter and, as they drew up outside an imposing building with enormous plate glass revolving doors and a marbled entrance hall full of important looking people hurrying to and fro, he began to have third ones as well.

'Mr Brown says nobody gets to see Sir Granville.'

'You know why that is?' said the driver knowledgeably. 'That's because Sir Granville blessed Holmes-Bottomley doesn't want to see them. I expect they all use the front door and then wonder why they get sent packing. I've met 'is sort before. You know what your best plan is?'

Paddington shook his head.

'You want to use the tradesmen's entrance and beard him in his den,' said the driver. 'Catch him unawares and don't take no for an answer. You mark my words. It's the only way to deal with them sort. If you like, I'll do a U-turn.'

Without waiting for a reply, he swung the cab round so that it was facing in the opposite direction, then he drove a little way down a narrow street towards the back of the building.

'There you go,' he said, as he stopped outside a small door marked PRIVATE. NO ADMITTANCE.

Paddington clambered out of the taxi, and after thanking the man for his advice and for helping him out with his heavily laden shopping basket on wheels, he waved goodbye.

'Thank you for your U-turn too,' he said gratefully. 'I've never done one of those before.'

'That's all right, guv'.' The driver opened the door leading to Sir Granville's offices. 'Best of luck. And if anyone asks you where you're going, 'old your nose and say you've come about the smell on the landing. It never fails.'

Pulling his basket behind him, Paddington made his way into the building. He had only gone a few feet when he heard a voice call out.

'And where do you think you're going young feller-me-bear?' asked a man in uniform from a small cubby-hole just inside the door.

'I've come about the smell on the landing,' said Paddington, taking a firm grip of his nose.

'Have you now?' said the man. 'And which landing might that be, may I ask?'

'I'm not sure,' said Paddington truthfully, 'but I think it may be the one right at the top of the building. The one

where Sir Granville has his office.'

At the mention of Sir Granville's name a change came over the doorkeeper.

'Oh, dear! Oh, dear!' he exclaimed, jumping into action. He reached for a telephone. 'Nobody tells me anything. You'd better 'urry. His nibs 'asn't arrived yet. He's late this morning, but I can tell you something for nothing. He won't want to be greeted by a smell on 'is landing when 'e does get 'ere, that's for sure. You'll find a lift just along to your right.'

Paddington needed no second bidding. He hurried along the corridor as fast as his legs would carry him and pressed the 'up' button before the man had a chance to change his mind.

'I'll let 'is secretary know you're coming,' called the doorkeeper as the doors slid shut.

Paddington had hardly got his breath back before there was a ping and doors opened again.

'Thank goodness you've got here in time.' A very superior looking lady dressed in a smart two-piece suit greeted him as he stepped out into a hall. She stared at him. 'I must say I wasn't expecting a bear.'

'Bears are good at smells,' said Paddington.

'I never knew that,' said the lady. 'How very interesting. I expect there were quite a lot where you come from,' she added disdainfully.

Paddington gave her a hard stare in return. 'It's very clean in Darkest Peru,' he exclaimed. 'It rains a lot up in the mountains.'

'Well, I don't know where you'd like to start,' said the lady. 'I can't tell where the smell's coming from myself. You're the expert.'

Paddington removed his paw from the end of his nose and gave a sniff. 'I think it may be coming from over there,' he announced, pointing towards a door which had Sir Granville Holmes-Bottomley's name painted on the outside.

'If you're going in there,' said the lady, eyeing Paddington's basket, 'I suggest you put your oranges in another room. Sir Granville has very sensitive nostrils.'

Paddington gazed about him as he followed the lady into Sir Granville's office. He had never been in such a large room before, nor one which had quite such thick carpet. Apart from a few pictures on the walls, which he didn't think very much of, and an enormous empty desk, there was nothing much else to be seen.

'Follow me.' The lady led the way towards an archway at the far end of the office. 'You can put your shopping basket in here,' she said. 'It's where Sir Granville keeps his shredder.'

'Sir Granville's got a shredder!' exclaimed Paddington. He peered excitedly at a large grey machine standing against one of the walls. 'Mrs Bird will be pleased.'

'Well, I don't know about Mrs Bird,' said the lady, 'but I have work to do, so I shall leave you to it.' With that she turned on her heels and disappeared from the room.

Left to his own devices, Paddington took a closer look at the shredder. He was most impressed, and it certainly seemed too good an opportunity to miss. He would be able to kill two birds with one stone. Not only could he surprise Sir Granville when he arrived by giving him the take-over bid, but if he worked quickly he could also surprise Mrs Bird by presenting her with a basketful of ready-sliced oranges. The Browns' housekeeper was always saying the worst part about making marmalade was cutting the oranges into chunks.

Opening a small drawer near the top of the machine, Paddington came across an instruction booklet. On the front there was a picture showing a girl pushing some pieces of paper through a slot in the top, and on the next page it showed the same girl watching some long strips of paper emerging from the bottom into a waste bucket. There were several warnings in red about how necessary it was for people with long hair to take extra care but, much to Paddington's relief, there was no mention of bears having to watch out for their whiskers. Nor, as far as he could see, was there anything about how to shred oranges, but he wasn't too disappointed. Paddington didn't think much of instruction books. Over the years he had often found they tended to leave out the very things you most wanted to know about. In fact, he was of the firm opinion that most of them were by people who never had to use the very machine they were describing.

It didn't take him long to discover the present booklet was no exception. It happened with the very first orange he tried to shred. For a start the slot was much too narrow for it to go through, and when he did finally manage to push it inside with the aid of one of Sir Granville's rulers and a pair of scissors, it simply disappeared, never to be seen again. Paddington tried a second orange and then a third, with exactly the same result. The only difference he could make out was that the noise of the motor was getting more and more muffled and from time to time there were strange gurgling sounds coming from somewhere deep inside the cabinet. Apart from a glassful or two of orange coloured dribbles falling into the bucket, even the juice was conspicuous by its absence.

Paddington was an optimistic bear at heart, but as he came at long last to the end of his supply of fruit, even he drew the line at the thought of going out to buy some

more. Climbing on top of a chair he peered down inside the slit, but there was nothing remotely like an orange anywhere in sight, let alone any chunks.

Far from looking anything at all like the smiling figure in the instruction booklet, Paddington's face grew longer and longer. He didn't dare think what Mrs Bird would say when she discovered all her oranges were missing; as for what Sir Granville would say when he tried to use his machine – it didn't bear thinking about.

As it happened, he didn't have long to wait for an answer to his second worry. He had only just settled down in a large chair behind the desk in order to await developments, when the door opened and a large man wearing a beard and a dark cloak entered the room. Paddington gazed in astonishment at the newcomer as first of all he removed the cloak, and then the beard. Suddenly he looked completely different.

Paddington jumped to his feet 'You must be the Scarlet Pimple!' he cried, pointing an accusing paw at the stranger.

The man nearly jumped out of his skin. 'What are you doing in my seat?' he bellowed. 'How dare you come in unannounced. I'm Sir Granville Holmes-Bottomley and . . .' he broke off and took a closer look at Paddington. 'That's a very good disguise you're wearing. May I ask where you bought it?'

'It's not a disguise,' said Paddington hotly. 'It's me, and I've come about the smell on the landing.'

'A bear?' repeated Sir Granville faintly. 'Come about the smell on the landing? And what was that you called me just now? The Scarlet Pimple?'

'It's not what *I* call you, Sir Scarlet . . . I mean Sir Granville,' said Paddington. 'Mr Brown says it's what everyone else in the City calls you.'

'Mr Brown?' Sir Granville stared at him. 'And who, pray, is Mr Brown when he's at home?'

Paddington felt in the bottom of his shopping basket. 'He lives at number thirty-two Windsor Gardens and he has something special for you. It's supposed to be given to you personally.'

Sir Granville took the envelope from Paddington and ran his thumb along inside the flap. As he opened it and gazed at the contents his face darkened.

'A take-over bid!' he exclaimed. 'I might have known! Well, I'll tell you what I do with things like this, bear.' He strode across the room towards the archway. 'I put them straight in my shredder.'

'I don't think you can, Sir Granville,' said Paddington unhappily, as he followed on behind. 'I'm afraid it's full of chunks.'

Sir Granville Holmes-Bottomley stopped dead in his tracks.

'Chunks?' he repeated. 'Did I hear you say my machine's full of *chunks?*'

'I thought I would shred some oranges for Mrs Bird while I was waiting,' explained Paddington. 'They may have to last us through the winter, so I bought rather a lot.'

Sir Granville passed a trembling hand across his brow as though in a dream, then he crossed to the window. 'I think I need some fresh air,' he said. 'It's getting rather hot in here. Is there anything else you feel I should know?'

'Well,' said Paddington, 'since you ask, a lot of people are having to do without their holidays this year because you won't give up the reins . . .'

Sir Granville held up his hand. 'One moment, bear,' he said. 'One thing at a time.' He reached forward and picked up his telephone. 'Tell my secretary,' he boomed, 'that under no circumstances am I to be disturbed.

'The floor is yours, bear!' he said, as he sat back in his chair. 'Now, begin at the beginning.'

Paddington took a deep breath. 'Well, Sir Granville,' he said. 'It all began when Mr Brown put some salt on his cornflakes this morning by mistake . . .'

Paddington spoke for a long time and when he had finished he felt very thirsty. 'If you don't mind, Sir Granville,' he announced, 'I think I'll have some juice out of your bucket.'

While he was gone Sir Granville reached across his desk and pressed a button.

Paddington arrived back in the office just as the

secretary came in. She stared at Paddington. 'I had no idea you were still here!' she exclaimed. 'I'll show you to the door.'

'Indeed you will do no such thing,' barked Sir Granville. 'This young bear has been an eye-opener to me.'

'Anyway,' said Paddington. 'There's no need to show me the door. I saw it when I came in.'

'You see what I mean,' said Sir Granville. 'Young Mr Brown has a whole new way of looking at things. It's a great pity there aren't more around like him. If I'm to be taken over I couldn't wish for it to be done in a nicer way.' Reaching for a pen, he added his signature with a flourish to the bottom of Mr Brown's document, then he handed it to Paddington.

'Perhaps if I ever take up the reins again,' he said wistfully, 'you would consent to being my right hand . . . er . . .'

'I don't think I've ever been anyone's right hand . . . er . . . before,' said Paddington. 'But I'm afraid I shan't be able to for a while. Mrs Bird's going to need help with her marmalade – especially when she sees what's happened to all the chunks. She may have to come here to make it.'

'I think,' said Sir Granville, 'I have an even better idea. Suppose I have my shredding machine sent over to Mrs Bird. It doesn't look as though I shall be needing it again for a while.'

To Paddington's surprise when he arrived back home all the Brown family were waiting to greet him and they gave a great cheer when he entered the room.

Mr Brown had already opened a bottle of champagne,

and Mrs Brown was busy with a pile of holiday brochures.

'Congratulations, Paddington,' said Mr Brown. 'I don't know what you did but, whatever it was, it worked. It's all over bar the shouting. Sir Granville has accepted the bid and he wants to see me in the morning. He says he's going to devote the rest of his life to doing good works.'

Judy held up an evening paper. 'It says here Sir Granville may even retire to the country and make marmalade.'

Paddington stared at the newspaper. To his surprise it had his picture on the front page. Above that, in large black letters were the words: BEAR HAS FIELD DAY IN CITY.

'What does that mean, Dad?' asked Jonathan.

'It's yet another of those financial expressions nobody outside the city really understands,' said Mr Brown. 'You see, on the Stock Exchange you have bulls and you have bears. Bulls are people who buy something cheaply and hope to sell it for a lot of money later on. Bears are people who sell something for a lot of money and hope to buy it back more cheaply some time in the future.'

'It sounds most complicated to me,' said Mrs Bird, 'I think it would be much simpler just to say you have bulls and you have bears, and then you have a bear called Paddington, and that's something different again. Nobody can ever guess what he's going to be up to next.'

'Mind you,' said Mr Brown, 'I'm not absolutely sure we've done the right thing. They do say there's a terrible smell in Sir Granville's building and no-one can find out where it's coming from. Have you any ideas, Paddington?'

Paddington gave Mr Brown a funny look.

'I think,' he announced hastily, 'I may go upstairs and have another bath. Working in the city makes you sticky.'

The Browns looked at each other in amazement as the door closed behind him.

'Wonders will never cease,' said Mrs Brown. 'Why on earth do you think he's doing that?'

'Perhaps,' said Mrs Bird wisely, 'it's best not to ask. If Paddington's having two baths in one day doesn't qualify for a special entry in the Guinness Book of Records, I don't know what does!'

The treasure hunt

LESLEY SMITH

> *There is nothing quite like a good treasure hunt, unless of course it's two treasure hunts!*
>
> MICHAEL BOND

It was a wonderful sunny late summer day in Bramble Wood. Harriet and Gruffy, Teddy bear twins, were lying on the grass amongst the buttercups by the Honeypot woodland store. Above the soft sound of humming bees they heard someone whistling happily.

They both sat up at once to see Patch, a rather scruffy looking Teddy bear, trundling along the pathway. He had a spade over his shoulder and carried a basket in the other hand.

'Hello Patch', smiled Harriet, tipping back her sun hat, 'where are you off to?'

'I'm going to dig for treasure in Scarecrow Field', he said proudly with a big smile on his face.

'Oh', said Gruffy, 'we've got nothing to do, can we come and help you?'

Patch said that it was a very good idea, and that he had plenty of lunch in his basket and a big bottle of lemonade to share with them.

So they all marched off along the winding path and over the stile at the edge of the wood.

In the field a tatty looking scarecrow stood sleepily in the sunshine. He couldn't speak, but he gave them a friendly wink.

'I think we'll start digging here,' said Patch. 'I feel that there is treasure around this place,' and he dug his spade into the stubbly ground. Then they all set to digging.

They had just started when a cheeky magpie flapped down. He hopped around tilting his head on one side. 'Haven't you got anything better to do on such a hot day than dig lots of holes?'

The three were too busy to bother with his silly remarks and just went on digging. Patch used the spade while Gruffy used his paws. Harriet busied herself clearing the stones out of the holes as they dug. The magpie tossed the stones all over the place.

Soon the sun got higher in the sky and the three friends became very hot. 'I'm tired', said Harriet, 'let's have a little rest.' 'We can have some lemonade', said Patch.

Gruffy wiped his paws on his dungarees and flopped onto the ground by the scarecrow with the others. The silly magpie flew onto the scarecrow's head and made fun of the bears.

'You'll never find treasure in this field,' he laughed and strutted up and down, flapping his wings and flicking his tail up and down.

The bears all looked very hot and dusty. Patch tugged at the cork of the

lemonade bottle. Suddenly the bottle fizzed and the cork shot out with a bang. It hit the scarecrow on the nose and frightened the magpie. With a screech the magpie jumped with surprise and took off into the skies, but as he flew away something shining fell out from under the scarecrow's hat. It was a gold ring.

Harriet gasped 'Why that's Mrs Nibble's ring! She lost it last week and has been looking everywhere for it.' Mrs Nibble was the rabbit who lived at the Honeypot Store. 'I wonder if the magpie took it,' said Gruffy. 'He seemed very smug. I bet that naughty magpie knew all about the ring and was just having a laugh at us', said Harriet.

They all decided to have a look under the hat to see if there was any more treasure. They had quite a surprise. 'That's a brass button from my trousers!' shouted Patch, 'And our Aunty Mabel's gold rimmed specs *and* our best marble, Gruffy,' said Harriet. 'Well, I think Magpie deserved the shock, the cork should have hit him in the nose.'

'Come on', said Gruffy, 'Let's go and show Mrs Nibble the ring'.

So the three bears packed up their lunch and hurried off to the Honeypot Store. Well! Mrs Nibble was surprised. She was so pleased when she saw the ring. 'You are good, honest children', she said, 'I caught that magpie in my kitchen last week. I must have taken the ring off to do my washing-up and forgot about it.'

Then Mrs Nibble took three brown paper bags and filled them with an apple each and sweets and some of her fresh baked biscuits.

'Well', said Patch, 'Who said we wouldn't find treasure in Scarecrow Field.' Then as they chatted on their way home Patch said. 'I think I might go digging for treasure again tomorrow.' Harriet and Gruffy groaned!

The bear who went to sea

KATE MARSHALL

> *Like Robert Louis Stevenson, Kate Marshall's Teddy believes in travel for travel's sake. The great thing is to be always on the move.*
>
> MICHAEL BOND

'Hullo,' said Lucy.

'Hullo,' said the bear.

'Oh dear,' said the wooden doll. 'I hope he won't be rough and noisy.'

'You'll like living here,' Lucy told the bear. 'There are lots of other toys to play with.'

'Oh yes,' said the wooden doll. 'But will *we* want to play with him? He looks rather wild.'

She gave a great sigh. But no one heard her.

Lucy and Teddy became the best of friends. Sometimes he would sit on Lucy's knee while she told him stories, and she often whispered secrets into his furry ears.

But he was always up to something. He chased the woolly lambs and he fought with the wooden soldiers. The animals in the toy farm ran off when they heard him coming. 'Cluck! Cluck!!' said the hens. 'Let's get out of his way!'

Teddy wasn't really a bad bear. He was always cheerful, and he meant to be good. But he liked lots of fun – and the other toys were so quiet.

'Come on, let's dance!' he said, picking up the wooden doll. He swung her round and round until her hat fell off, and so did her shoes, and she cried, 'Please stop! You're making me dizzy!' And then one of her wooden legs fell off.

'You bad bear!' Lucy was very cross when she saw what had happened to the poor little doll. 'I'll have to mend her right away.'

Teddy sulked. It wasn't his fault. Why blame him?

While Lucy mended her doll, he sat in the corner. But even then he was up to mischief. Lucy didn't see him drawing on the wall with a crayon he had found on the floor.

Lucy's doll was soon as good as new. Lucy gave her a hug and put her to bed.

Then she saw what Teddy had done. 'Just look at the wall!' she cried. 'Oh, Teddy, you are very naughty.'

'Not my fault,' he growled from the corner.

None of the toys would play with Teddy after that.

'You're much too rough,' they said.

So Teddy found a ball and began to kick it about, all by himself.

'This isn't much fun,' he said. 'I'm so bored.'

But then he looked out of the window and saw Lucy setting off for a walk. 'She's going out,' he said to himself.

'Now's my chance. I'll run away!'

He called to the little black cat. 'Let's go off together and look for adventure.'

'Good idea!' said the cat who was tired of prowling along the rooftops at night.

So paw in paw they set off for the sea shore.

'Look what I see!' said Teddy.

'A box?' said the cat.

'A boat,' said the bear. 'We can make it into a boat. All we need is a piece of cloth for a sail. Wait there! I know where I can find just what we want.' And he rushed back home.

He found a piece of canvas in the garden shed, a stout pole and a length of rope.

'What are you doing?' asked the other toys.

'I'm building a boat – I'm going to sea!' said Teddy, and they all stared at him in amazement.

Before long, he had rigged up a sail and fixed it to the box. 'You *are* clever,' said the cat. 'What a clever bear you are!'

'Yes, I am,' said Teddy (who was a little boastful). 'Now let's set sail!'

They pushed the boat out from the shore. A light breeze caught the sail. 'We're off!' shouted Teddy. 'Ship ahoy!'

A huge fish gaped at them. Whatever next!

'This is splendid,' said Teddy, and he began to sing. The cat wasn't too certain – she didn't like getting her paws wet. And there really wasn't much room on the boat. And what would they do when they got hungry?

'Leave it to me,' said the bear, and he went on singing in a rather tuneless voice.

When Lucy came back from her walk, the other toys told her what had happened.

'He's building a boat!'

'He says he's going to sail away!'

'The cat's gone too – both of them in one boat!'

'Oh dear, oh dear!' Lucy rushed down to the shore. Far away in the distance, she could see the little boat tossing on the waves, and she could hear singing. Teddy waved a paw to her.

'Come back! Come back!' she cried, but it was too late.

Soon the little breeze turned to a strong gust of wind that whipped up the waves. 'Oh,' said the cat, looking at the sky, 'It's going to rain!'

'Don't worry – leave it all to me. We'll be as right as rain,' said Teddy. And with that, a huge wave tipped the little boat over and the two were left splashing in the water.

'Oh, how wet it is!' gasped the poor cat.

They bobbed and tossed in the water for what seemed like ages –

and then suddenly Teddy gasped, 'The shore! I can see the shore!' A huge wave swept the toys along and they found themselves hurtled on to a sandy beach.

'We're safe anyway!' said Teddy.

The cat could hardly speak. 'But we're so cold and wet and hungry, and far from home!' She gave a great sob. 'Oh, I wish we were safely back home!'

Teddy wished the same, but he didn't say so. After all, it was his adventure.

The toys huddled together and at last they fell asleep. Next morning when they woke, the cat's fur was almost dry. She twitched her whiskers, and said, 'I'm off. I'm going to look for help.'

'No,' said Teddy. 'You wait there. I'll go and explore.'

He hadn't gone far when he found a toy engine left on the shore. 'Well, this is a piece of luck!' he said.

He climbed in and drove back along the shore towards the cat. 'Toot! toot!' he called. 'Here I am. We can travel much faster this way.'

The cat was looking out for him.

'What do you think?' she said. 'We aren't on a lonely island after all. Look!' and she pointed to the roofs of the town and the spire of the church. 'We've been washed up in the next bay – we can't be far from home.'

'All aboard,' shouted Ted, and they set off in the little engine.

'I know!' said Teddy after a minute or two. 'There's the pier. And there's the ice cream kiosk. We're not far from home.' He knew just where they were because Lucy often took him to play on the sands.

They left the little engine on the shore, since it might belong to someone, and they set off up the path towards home.

When they reached their own street and their own house, the cat began to purr. 'It's good to be home.' She climbed on Teddy's back and pressed the bell.

'I hope Lucy won't be cross,' she said.

'Oh, no,' said Teddy, but he wasn't at all sure about that. 'Oh, dear, I'm sore and stiff.'

'So am I,' said the cat, 'and I've hurt my head.'

When Lucy saw the two weary travellers, she wasn't a bit cross. 'You're back! You're safe!' she cried. There was a hug for Teddy and a special pat for the cat.

She put them both to bed and bandaged them up, and the little wooden doll, who had quite forgiven Teddy, brought them supper.

'I'm not going on an adventure again,' said Teddy.

'Nor am I,' said the cat.

'Fancy us going to sea, though,' said Teddy. 'I bet I'm the first bear that's ever been to sea.' And he began humming, 'Yo, ho, ho . . .'

'Do be quiet,' said the cat, 'and go to sleep.'

But Teddy didn't go to sleep right away. He was too busy planning how, next day, he would tell the toy soldiers and the woolly lambs and the farm animals, all about his great adventure. And then he wondered – where should he go next?

What can I do today?

ELIZABETH BROOK

> *'What can I do today?' is a call which must strike many a chord in people's minds. Who hasn't uttered it from time to time? No one can say that Elizabeth Brook's story of Teddy Tum Tum is short of ideas.*
>
> MICHAEL BOND

'What can I do today?' said Teddy Tum Tum, as he dipped his spoon into his boiled egg. 'It's a fine sunny morning. There are lots of things to do outdoors.'

He thought for a moment. 'I could go and play cricket. I could weed the garden. I could catch a bus to the seaside.' He looked across at the wooden duck on the bedside table. 'What would you do?'

'Quack,' said the duck. 'Quack, quack.'

'What a good idea!' said Tum Tum. 'I'll go on the river. I'll hire a rowing boat.'

So he hopped out of bed and dressed as quickly as he could. He sang a little song. 'I'm off to the river, hooray, hooray. I'm off to the river today.'

He took cushions to sit on and a floppy hat to keep the sun out of his eyes. He took a book to read and sandwiches to eat at lunchtime. And so he set off towards the river.

But Tum Tum didn't notice that the black clouds were gathering and the wind was rising. Then the first drops of rain began to fall.

'Never mind,' he said to himself. 'Won't be much rain. I'm sure of that.'

By the time he reached the river, it was raining steadily. The boats were tied up, and the man in the boathouse shook his head. "Tisn't weather for boating, sir.' He pointed to the sky. 'Going to be a real storm. Come back when it's sunny.'

So Tum Tum trudged back along the path. He ate his sandwiches at home, looking glumly out of the window at the rain.

Next morning, it was still rather dull and cloudy. 'I won't go on the river today,' said Tum Tum. 'I'll think of something else to do.'

First he sailed his toy boat in the bath. Then he splashed happily among the bubbles.

'What can I do today?' he thought. 'I'll go swimming. That's what I'll do. I'll go to the baths.'

He was quite a good swimmer and could swim the whole length of the baths.

'I'm off to the baths, hooray, hooray. I'm off to the baths today,' he sang.

He took his swimming costume and a few biscuits to eat when he'd finished his swim.

But when he got to the baths, there was a big notice 'CLOSED'.

'That's right,' said a man nearby. 'Closed for today. It's a holiday. Open again tomorrow.'

'Oh dear,' said Tum Tum, and he turned and went home again. He put his swimming costume back in the cupboard and ate the biscuits.

Next morning was bright and sunny. The garden looked at its very best. Tum Tum sniffed the air and wondered what he should do. 'I won't go on the river. I won't go to the baths,' he said. 'I know! I'll bake cakes and ask my cousins to tea. We can play hide and seek in the shrubbery and rounders on the grass.'

'Hooray, hooray, it's baking day today,' he sang.

So he got everything out of the cupboard ready to begin baking – flour and margarine and sugar and eggs and a lemon and cocoa and icing sugar and jam, as well as scales and a big mixing bowl, and wooden spoons.

He made scones and chocolate cakes, and little sponge cakes, each with a cherry on top. He made a big sponge with jam in the middle and white icing on top. He decorated the cake with a marzipan heart and stuck cherries round about. One cherry fell off, and he popped it into his mouth. 'That is a splendid cake,' he beamed, 'even though I say it myself.'

By this time it was very hot in the kitchen and Tum Tum sat down and mopped his brow with his handkerchief.

'What a feast!' he said.

'How pleased they'll be!'

Off he went to the 'phone to ring his cousins and ask them to tea.

'Hullo, Tum Tum,' said Auntie. 'How are you?'

'I've been very busy,' he replied. 'I've made scones and cakes and all sorts of good things. Can Barney and Betty and Billy come to tea?'

'Oh, I'm sorry,' said Auntie. 'They've gone to the seaside to see Uncle Bruin. They won't be back till tomorrow.'

'Never mind,' said Tum Tum, and he put down the 'phone feeling very disappointed.

'Here's a lovely day and lots to eat,' he said to himself. 'I could have gone to the river. I could have gone to the baths. Oh dear!' And he began to feel a little sorry for himself.

He wandered out of the house into the garden and down the path. He looked up and down the road. There was no one around but Raggity Peg, the doll next door, swinging on the gate to her home.

'Hullo, Peg!' he called. 'What are you doing today?'

'Nothing much,' she said, and he thought the doll seemed a little sad. 'And I'll tell you something. It's my birthday.'

'Well!' said Tum Tum. 'Many happy returns. Listen, would you like to come to tea? I've got lots of scones and little cakes and a very special big cake.'

'Oh, yes,' said Peg. 'Thank you.'

'We'll have tea in the garden,' said Tum Tum. 'By the shed. At four o'clock.'

Raggity Peg arrived in her best dress with new ribbons

in her hair. Tum Tum had spread out a bright checked table cloth. On it he laid the cups and saucers and plates and cakes and scones and other good things.

'Oooh!' said Raggity Peg. 'What a party!'

They couldn't eat all the marzipan heart cake, so Tum Tum wrapped it up for Peg to take home. 'Have the last little cake,' he said. 'Or an apple.' There was still lots left over.

'I couldn't eat another thing,' she said.

It was much too hot to run about and play, so they sang all the songs they knew and told jokes and riddles and last of all, Teddy Tum Tum sang 'Happy Birthday to you', and gave Peg a flower to wear.

'It's been a good day after all,' he said to himself, as he washed up the cups and saucers and plates.

'Now, what can I do tomorrow?'

Grizzwold

S Y D   H O F F

> *Grizzwold is a very fine name for a bear, but in his*
> *search for somewhere nice to live he nearly ends*
> *up as a Grizzwas.*
>
> M I C H A E L   B O N D

In the far North lived a bear named Grizzwold.

Grizzwold was so big three rabbits could sit in his footprint.

Other bears had no trouble going into caves to sleep.
Grizzwold always got stuck.

One morning there was a loud noise in the forest.
All the other bears ran away.

Grizzwold went to see what it was.
He saw men chopping down trees.

'Timber!' they shouted.

'What's the big idea?' asked Grizzwold. 'What are you doing in my forest?'

'We are sorry,' said the men. 'We have to send these logs down the river to the mill. They will be made into paper.'

'I can't live in a forest with no trees,' said Grizzwold.
He went to look for a new place to live.
Grizzwold looked until he saw houses.
'What can I do here?' he asked.

'You can be a bearskin rug,' said some people.
Grizzwold lay down on the floor.
The people stepped all over him.
'Ow! I don't like this,' said Grizzwold.
He left the house.

Grizzwold saw people going to a dance. The people wore masks.

Grizzwold went to the dance too.

'You look just like a real bear,' said the people.

'Thank you,' said Grizzwold.

The people started to dance.

Grizzwold started to dance too.

'It is time to take off our masks,' said somebody.

All the people took off their masks.

'Take off yours too,' they said to Grizzwold.

'I can't,' he said. 'This is my real face.'

'You don't belong here,' said the people. 'You belong in the zoo.'

Grizzwold went to the zoo.

The bears were begging for peanuts.

Grizzwold begged too.

'Please don't stay,' said the bears. 'We need all the peanuts we get. Try the circus.'

Grizzwold went to the circus.
They put skates on him. He went FLOP!
They put him on a bicycle. He went CRASH!
'I suppose it takes practice,' said Grizzwold.
'It certainly does,' said the trained bears.
He ran until he came to a nice forest.
'I'm glad to be here,' he said.
'We are very glad you are here too,' said some hunters.
They took aim.

'Don't shoot!' said a game warden. 'This is a game reserve. No guns allowed.'

The hunters left.

'Thank you,' said Grizzwold.

'You will be safe here,' said the warden.

'People cannot shoot animals here. They can only take pictures.'

All the people wanted to take Grizzwold's picture. He was the biggest bear they had ever seen.

They gave him all the peanuts he could eat.

'This is the life for me,' said Grizzwold.

He was very happy.

Teddy's story

ROSE IMPEY AND SUE PORTER

> *Take one bear out for a walk in the woods, a wicked witch, a remote castle and one egg long past its sell-by date. Mix them all together. The result is a splendidly fast-moving tale in the classical tradition.*
>
> MICHAEL BOND

Grandma, can we have a story?

What kind of story?

A story from the storybag.

All right, let's see who's inside today . . .

We'll call this 'Teddy's story'.

One fine day, not so very long ago, a Teddy set out to see the world. He wore a velvet cloak and a golden crown which shone in the sun.

He looked like a brave prince, but he wasn't.

Teddy loved to dress up and pretend. Sometimes this got him into trouble.

As he walked along, Teddy whistled a tune.

He didn't notice that 'someone' was hiding behind a tree, watching him.

It was a wicked Witch and if there ever was a wicked Witch it was this one.

'Ha ha ha ha! A handsome prince,' she said. 'Exactly what I'm looking for.'

'But I'm not really a prince,' said Teddy.

'You look like a prince to me,' said the Witch. 'I shall put you under a spell and lock you up for a hundred years, or more if I feel like it.'

Without another word, she carried him away.

They flew on the wind until they came to a tall castle, hidden deep in the dark, dark woods.

The witch took Teddy to the very top of the castle and locked him in.

Now Teddy was in real trouble. There was no way to escape. He could only wave for help and hope someone might pass by and see him.

Quite by chance, someone did pass by. Doll was on the way to visit her grandma, who lived on the edge of the dark, dark woods.

When she saw Teddy waving for help, Doll began to search for a way in to rescue him. Soon she found a hole leading down into a tunnel. It was slimy and grimy underground, but Doll kept on bravely to the end of the tunnel where she found a door. Opening it a crack, Doll slipped through and found herself in the Witch's kitchen.

The Witch was stirring a cauldron, which bubbled like thick porridge on the stove.

She was chanting a spell,

As Doll crept past, she took one of the Witch's eggs out of a box on the table. 'Teddy might be hungry,' she thought. Then she raced up the steep stairs to the very top of the castle.

When Doll unlocked the door, she found Teddy lying asleep on the bed, dreaming. She tiptoed across the room and kissed him on the end of his nose.

'Who are you?' said Teddy, waking up and blushing.

But there was no time for Doll to explain.

Already they could hear the Witch's hard little feet climbing the stone staircase. Now they were both in trouble.

'Oh dear,' said Teddy, 'what are we going to do?'

Doll reached in her pocket and took out the egg.

Doll rolled the egg towards the door. She hoped the Witch might trip over it and give them a chance to escape. But this was a magic egg. As it rolled, it grew bigger and bigger. When it reached the door it split in two with a loud, 'Craaacck!'

Out leaped a Monster with needle-sharp teeth. The Monster opened his mouth wide and roared. 'HHRRRAAARRGHGH!' The whole castle shook.

The Witch was terrified. She ran downstairs and kept on running until she was very far away.

At first Doll and Teddy were frightened too. But Monster told them how the wicked Witch had captured him many years ago and trapped him inside the egg.

'You helped me to escape,' he told Doll.

'What can I do for you?'

'Would you take us home?' said Doll. 'My grandma will have tea ready.' And Doll and Teddy climbed onto Monster's back.

As they sailed over the dark, dark woods towards her grandma's house, Doll said to Teddy, 'Wait till my

grandma sees that I've brought a brave and handsome prince to tea.'

Teddy smiled. He felt like a handsome prince.

'You may kiss my paw,' he said. But Doll kissed his nose instead.

The bears of the air

ARNOLD LOBEL

When Grandfather Bear sets out to teach his four grandchildren the things all young bears should know, the tables are turned, and he ends up a little older and wiser himself.

MICHAEL BOND

Ronald, Donald, Harold, and Sam were four bears.

They lived in a cave with their old grandfather.

Grandfather had a book.

He would often read to them.

'A good bear should go for walks, take naps, catch fish, and climb up and down trees,' read Grandfather.

The small bears tried hard to do all of the things in Grandfather's book.

But when Ronald climbed trees he would get splinters in his nose.

When Donald took naps he always had bad dreams.

When Harold went for walks his toes would freeze and snow would fall down on him.

And Sam fell in the water every time he tried to catch fish.

'Things a good bear should do are not much fun,' said Ronald, Donald, Harold, and Sam.

'Nonsense,' said Grandfather. 'I will show you how.'

'This is the way to catch fish,' said Grandfather.

But Ronald and Donald were not listening.

Ronald practised juggling Donald in the air, and Donald began to do somersaults. In no time at all he somersaulted very well.

'Ridiculous,' grumbled Grandfather.

'This is the way to take naps,' said Grandfather.

But Harold and Sam were not listening. Harold found some rope. He made a lasso and perfected rope tricks.

Sam carved a violin out of a piece of wood. He soon learned to play beautifully.

'Impossible,' growled Grandfather.

The bears were very happy with their new accomplishments.

They stretched a wire between two trees and became fine acrobats.

'What are you doing up there?' shouted Grandfather.

'We are bears of the air, and we have found some things to do that are fun,' sang Sam as he played his violin.

Grandfather was angry. 'Come down at once,' he said.

That night the bears were punished. They were sent to bed without their supper.

'There is nothing in my book about rope tricks or juggling or somersaults or violins,' said Grandfather as he ate a boiled potato.

'This is the way to take walks,' explained Grandfather the next morning.

'Today we will have tree-climbing, nap-taking, and fish-catching lessons. These are useful things for a bear to do.'

'This is the way to climb trees,' instructed Grandfather.

Just then Grandfather bumped into a bird's nest.

'You clumsy old bear!' screeched the bird who lived in the nest. 'You are scrambling my eggs!'

The bird was so angry that she snatched Grandfather's glasses.

'Help! My glasses! Stop, thief!' cried Grandfather.

'Never fear . . .' said Harold as he threw his lasso and caught the bird with the loop—

'the bears of the air . . .' said Ronald as he juggled Donald over his head—

'will get those glasses back,' said Donald as he somersaulted high up to the bird and quickly grabbed Grandfather's glasses.

Then Sam played a song on his violin. The bird stopped screeching.

'What beautiful music,' she said with a sigh.

'My little eggs will hear it and they will soon hatch happily!'

The bird flew back to her nest and fell asleep.

Grandfather was delighted to have his glasses back on his nose again.

After that, Grandfather only used his book to sit down on while he watched his grandsons juggling and lassoing and somersaulting and violining.

He decided that these were fine and useful things for good bears to do.

Bluff and Bran
and the tree house

MEG RUTHERFORD

> *Bran is a very unprotesting bear, which is perhaps just as well, for with a cat like Bluff for a friend he doesn't get much time to complain.*
>
> MICHAEL BOND

Bluff and Bran spent the night beside a large soft cushion. At sunrise Bluff rolled over, and felt the sun warming the pale fur on her tummy.

She got up and went from window to window to see what kind of a day it was. There wasn't a cloud in the sky. It looked perfect.

But Bluff was hungry. She played a wild noisy game in a paper bag to let the little girl know that she wanted breakfast.

After breakfast, she and Bran had a little rest.

Then, as it was far too nice a day to be indoors, Bluff began to drag Bran towards the cat-flap. She was determined to take him to the treehouse.

She squeezed

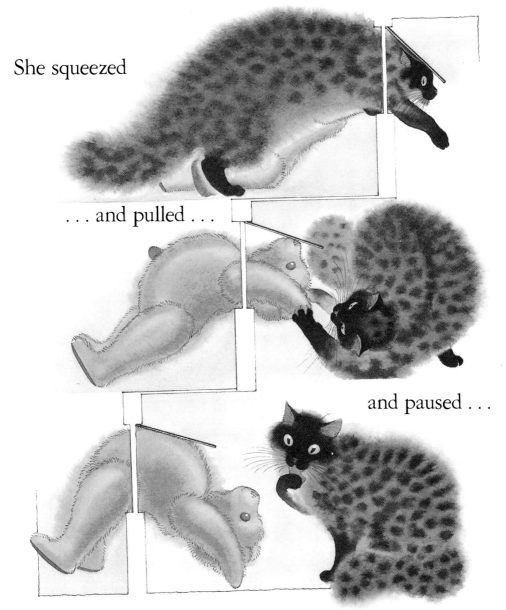

. . . and pulled . . .

and paused . . .

and PULLED again . . . and POP! they were outside, in the bright blue beautiful day.

Bluff tugged and bumped Bran across the garden, helping him over the rough patches when stones rubbed his back and plants caught his arms and legs. At last they reached the foot of the tree . . . where they got stuck! But help was coming.

'There you are,' said the little girl, out of breath with running. 'I've been looking for you everywhere.'

She took them up to the treehouse. 'You'll be nice and safe up here,' she said, 'and I'll be home in time for tea.' She fixed a safety net, and went away.

Soon a gusty wind blew up, so Bluff didn't hear the squirrel when he came into the treehouse and began to climb all over Bran.

Bran found him rather tickly.

When Bluff turned and saw the squirrel, she flew at him . . . and bumped the chair so hard that Bran shot out of the door and into the net!

The squirrel escaped up the rope . . . but poor Bran was circling in mid-air.

First he went ROUND one way, then he went ROUND the other.

He saw birds flying at him as he hung upside down. It was all very muddling.

Bluff squeezed past the chair which was jammed in the doorway, and, clinging by her claws, came down the tree to see how she could rescue Bran.

As she reached the ground there was a flash of lightning and a BOOM of thunder.

Everything was very still and frightening.

She leapt to save Bran.

But her weight shook the treehouse, and the chair came tumbling down on top of them.

Bluff ran for cover!

She watched and waited till she was sure that nothing else would fall.

It was raining now, big soft drops were thudding onto Bran.

Bluff ran back and sprang again for Bran, just as thunder BOOMED.

Then lightning struck the treehouse! There was a splintering crash and it came hurtling down, smashing into smithereens.

Slowly the storm moved away, and the rain stopped, the last drops glistening on the trees nearby.

It was quiet again in the garden.

As the sun came out, Bluff wriggled from the wreckage and pulled Bran free.

Then she saw the squirrel, and remembered how cross she was with him. Leaving Bran to get used to being the right way up, she chased the squirrel, just to show him what she thought of him.

The squirrel didn't wait to hear. He ran away.
Bluff gave up the chase, wanting to be back with Bran.
With a flick of her paws she shook him out of the net,
then gently took him home.

And that's where the little girl found them, when she
came home.

Bozzy finds a friend

GRAHAM J. BROOKS

> *Anyone who has ever endured the ignominy of being the last one in the crowd to be chosen for someone's team, will understand how Bozzy must have felt when he was befriended.*
>
> MICHAEL BOND

Bozzy was a very sad bear. Nobody loved him. All day long he would sit at the bottom of the big toy box, squashed by the weight of the big fat hippo.

Poor Bozzy had one eye missing with just a tuft of thread left where it should be. His coat was bare because a lot of his fur had fallen out, especially on his nose where he'd been dragged along upside down.

Every morning when the children came into school they chose their toys from the big toy box. The dolls were always favourites and lots of the children wanted the cars. The big red train never had to wait long before someone picked him up, and even the fat hippo was sometimes taken out of the box. But no one ever chose Bozzy.

All day long he could hear the children's voices. He wished he could be out there playing with them.

One day when all the children had gone outside, he heard the teacher talking to someone. Bozzy stood on tiptoe in the empty box, but he was just too short to see over the edge.

'I know, Emily,' the teacher said. 'Let's find you a toy and then you can go outside to play with the other children.'

Bozzy heard the teacher walking towards him, so he quickly sat down in the corner of the box.

'Oh dear, there's only one left,' said the teacher. 'It'll have to do.'

Before Bozzy knew what was happening, he was being lifted out of the toy box by one ear, which only just stayed on. He was very excited. At last he was going to play with someone!

'Here you are Emily,' said the teacher. 'You can have this bear. He's a bit ragged but never mind.'

The little girl took Bozzy in her arms and hugged him.

Bozzy couldn't believe it. This was just what he had always wanted, someone to love him. So he hugged her back as hard as he could. He was only a little bear, so it wasn't a very big hug and he was not even sure if she knew.

'Now, Emily, off you go with the other children,' said the teacher.

So they went outside, on to the playing field. The other children were playing games, running, shouting and laughing, in fact so busy no one noticed Emily and Bozzy.

Emily sat down on the grass with Bozzy. She told him it was her first day at her new school and she felt very strange and lonely. She told him all about her mummy, daddy and her little brother Michael who was too young for school.

Then it was Bozzy's turn. He told Emily how he had

once been a very handsome bear. He'd belonged to a big family of children. But one by one they'd grown up and they didn't play with him any more. He was given away and that was how he ended up in the toy box.

Before they knew it, the teacher was calling them in. Bozzy sat with Emily all afternoon. When it was time to go home the teacher said to Emily, 'Would you like to take your bear home with you? You seem to be getting on so well together, and no one ever plays with him. You can look after each other!'

Emily's mummy was waiting for her outside the school gates. Immediately, Emily cried, 'Mummy, look at Bozzy – he's my new friend. But he's lost one eye. Can we give him a new one?'

'I'm sure we can find one,' her mother said. 'Maybe we can fix his ear as well.'

Emily skipped all the way home. After tea, they set to work mending Bozzy. First they found a button for his eye. It was only a little smaller than the other one and Mummy sewed it on. Then they stitched his ear and last of all they gave him a bath. Bozzy wasn't too sure about that at first, but once he was in the water he enjoyed it, even if the scrubbing tickled.

What a difference it made! He could see properly once more and, with his fur fluffed up, his bare patches were nearly covered. He really was quite a handsome bear.

Next day at school Emily waved goodbye to her mother and went into the playground proudly carrying Bozzy. At first no one noticed her but then another little girl spotted Bozzy.

'That's a lovely bear,' she said.

'Yes,' said Emily, 'this is Bozzy. If you're very careful you can hold him.' She handed Bozzy to the girl who stroked him gently.

One by one the other children noticed him. They began to gather round Emily and her special bear. Everyone admired Bozzy and his fine coat, and they all wanted a turn of holding him.

And Bozzy loved all the attention after so long sitting alone in the toy box. He looked quite different now, happy and cheerful and not sad any more.

Emily soon got to know the other children and made lots of friends. She put Bozzy back in the toy box so that the others could play with him too. From that day on he was always a great favourite and never again did the fat hippo sit on him.

'What a fine bear!' everyone said.

'He's a *very* special bear,' said Emily.

How Bruiny came to live next door

ENID BLYTON

> Enid Blyton has opened more doors to the joy of reading than most people, so good for her; or Jolly good in this case.
>
> MICHAEL BOND

One day Jolly went down to the town to get a pot of black-currant jam for Tiptoe, and he found everyone really most excited.

'The toy fort is finished at last!' cried Mr To-and-Fro, the wobbly man. 'Look – isn't it grand?'

Jolly looked. On the top of the hill on the other side of the town was a fine toy fort. It was made of wood, and was

painted red and white. It had four towers, one at each end, and a draw-bridge that could be let up and down by chains, for soldiers to march over when they wanted to go in or out of the fort.

'That's for all the toy soldiers in Toyland!' said the pink cat. 'You know, they've had to live in ordinary

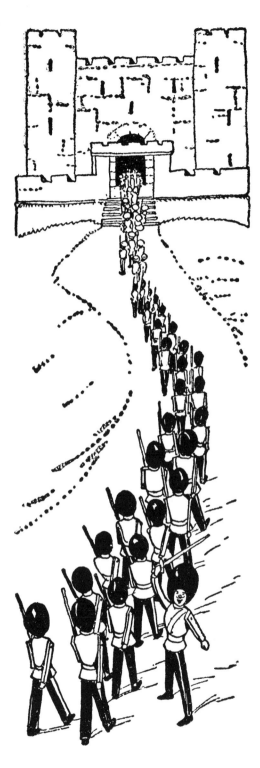

houses up to now, because there wasn't a proper fort for them to live in. But now one has been built, and there it is! Soon all the soldiers everywhere will march up the hill into the fort!'

'It's a marvellous fort,' said Jolly. 'Dear me – I wonder if the wooden soldiers who live next to us will have to go too. How we shall miss them! They are so smart and polite and kind.'

Jolly ran home to tell Tiptoe. He was just in time to see the soldiers who lived next door marching out in line, their captain at their head.

'We're off to live at the fort!' said the Captain proudly. 'The lead soldiers are going to live there too. So all the soldiers will live together now, in a proper fort, and we shall be able to guard Toyland well.'

'Tiptoe! Come and say good-bye to the soldiers!' cried Jolly. 'They're going!'

Tiptoe ran out. She shook hands with all the soldiers. Then she and Jolly thought it would be fun to go with them and see them march over the draw-bridge into the fort. So they ran beside them, down the hill, through the streets of the town, and up the hill beyond. The draw-bridge was let down, of course, and hundreds of toy soldiers of all kinds were marching over it into the grand toy fort.

A band stood nearby playing them into the fort. 'Tan-tan-tara!' went the trumpets. 'Rub-a-dub-dub, dub-dub, dub-dub!' went the drums. It was all most exciting.

When the soldiers were safely in the fort, the draw-bridge was pulled up. Now nobody could get in or out. The soldiers stood in their places, saluted, and then marched about when their captains shouted orders.

'We *shall* miss the soldiers next door!' sighed Tiptoe. 'They were so nice, and I did feel so safe with such a lot of brave men nearby. Let's go and call on Josie, Click, and Bun, Jolly.'

The two of them set off to the little Tree-house – but on the way they met Bruiny, the little brown teddy-bear, and he was crying bitterly. He had a big red handkerchief up to his eyes, and he didn't see Tiptoe and Jolly. He walked straight into them, bump!

'Bruiny! Whatever's the matter?' cried Tiptoe, in alarm. 'Have you hurt yourself?'

'No, but something has hurt my house,' said Bruiny. 'Come and see.'

He took them to where his little brick-house had been, and there it was, all knocked down.

'I am sure one of those great big clumsy rocking-horses has been along this way,' sobbed Bruiny. 'And he must have rocked himself over my dear little house. That's the worst of those rocking-horses – they're so big that they just don't look where they're going!'

'Come and get some more bricks to build a new house,' said Tiptoe, taking his hand.

'No. I'm not going to have bricks this time,' said Bruiny, wiping his eyes. 'I've heard that you can build houses of cards. Did you know that? So I'm going to build myself a house of snap-cards. I can get some in the town, I know. Come along and help me.'

Well, it wasn't long before the three of them had a pack of snap-cards. They were rather big and heavy to carry, so Tiptoe and Jolly took some too. They chose a nice open spot in a field where toy sheep were eating the grass, and began to build a card-house. You know how to build one, don't you? Well, that's just how the three of them built Bruiny's!

First they leaned two cards against one another, and then they put two cards against the sides. Then two cards against the edges of those, and then two more cards flat on top. That was the first room. Then they built the next room on top of that, just the same. It was most exciting.

When there were four rooms, and the house of cards was quite high, Bruiny said the house was big enough.

'One room shall be the kitchen – the bottom one,' he said. 'The next shall be my sitting-room. The next shall be

my bedroom, and the topmost of all shall be my spare-room. Isn't it a lovely house?'

Well, Tiptoe and Jolly thought it didn't look a very comfortable kind of house, but they didn't like to say so. Bruiny asked them to go into the kitchen. So they squashed in between the cards – and alas, Bruiny pushed too hard! Down fell the whole of the card-house, swish-swish-swish!

So it all had to be built up again. It didn't take long, of course. This time Jolly said they wouldn't go inside because it really was time for them to go home to dinner.

'Well, thank you for helping me,' said the little bear, smiling. 'It's a nice house, isn't it? I shall go and buy myself some furniture for it now. So good-bye. Isn't it funny – there isn't a front door to lock!'

Bruiny went off to the town, and Tiptoe and Jolly went home. They sat down and had a good dinner, for they were hungry. They had a lot to talk about. First they talked about the soldiers all going to live at the fort, and how sad they were not to have them next door any more. Then they talked about poor Bruiny, and how his house had got knocked down, and how they hoped that his house of cards would be all right.

'It's got no stairs. How do you think he'll go up to bed?' asked Jolly.

'We didn't put a chimney,' said Tiptoe. 'Where will the smoke go if he lights a fire?'

'Bruiny is rather a stupid little bear, though he is a darling,' said Tiptoe. 'He wants somebody to look after him, *I* think.'

All that day Tiptoe and Jolly were busy, taking down their old curtains and putting up clean ones, and taking out their little mats to beat the dust from them. They forgot about the soldiers and the card-house. But as they were sitting down to supper, they heard the sound of soft footsteps. Then they heard the sound of somebody crying, and a knock on the door. Jolly opened it.

Outside stood Bruiny the bear, crying into his red handkerchief again. 'Can I come in?' he asked. 'I've nowhere to sleep tonight, and I'm very, very unhappy.'

'Oh, Bruiny dear! Of course you can come in!' cried Tiptoe.

'Come and share our supper. What has happened to your dear little card-house?'

'A lot of things happened to it,' said poor Bruiny, wiping his eyes, and looking more cheerful when he saw a nice supper on the table. 'First of

all, Mr To-and-Fro came to call, and he wobbled against the walls and knocked the whole house down. So I had to build it up again.'

'Poor Bruiny!' said Jolly, pouring the bear out some cocoa. 'Go on.'

'Well, then I tried to get a wardrobe up into the bedroom, but we forgot the stairs, you know – so I had to throw it up – and it knocked the house down again,' went on Bruiny.

Tiptoe felt as if she wanted to laugh, but she didn't like to.

'Then the rain came and made the cards go soft and wet,' said Bruiny, 'and I had to throw them away and build the house from other cards in the pack. I can tell you I felt pretty tired!'

'Poor Bruiny!' said Tiptoe again. 'Eat your sausage-roll. You'll feel better then.'

'Well, I got a new card-house built again, and went into the kitchen to have a rest,' said Bruiny. 'And I fell fast asleep. And suddenly I woke up in a dreadful fright! The house was falling about my ears! Swish-swish – it all fell down. And do you know why? It was because the silly toy sheep in the field had bumped against it in the dark!'

'Never mind, Bruiny,' said Jolly, a great idea coming into his head. 'I've got a fine plan! The house next door is empty, because the wooden soldiers have all gone to live in the fort. What about *you* living there, next to us? Then Tiptoe can look after you a bit, and we can all have fun together!'

Well, Bruiny was so happy that he swallowed a whole

sausage-roll at once, and choked. It really was a marvellous idea.

And the next day Bruiny moved into the soldiers' old cottage, and hung up pretty curtains of blue. Tiptoe and Jolly helped him, and the clockwork clown came over too, very pleased that old Bruiny was going to live so near.

'Well, this *is* a bit of luck!' said Bruiny, when the house was finished and a kettle was singing on his toy stove. 'A nice little house – and nice little friends next door! I *am* glad my old house was knocked down flat!'

And that is how Bruiny came to live next-door to Tiptoe and Jolly. Won't they all have fun together?

Teddy Robinson keeps house

JOAN G. ROBINSON

> *Teddy Robinson becomes a bear of property; an early settler in what nowadays we would call 'Cardboard City'.*
>
> MICHAEL BOND

One day Teddy Robinson sat on the kitchen-table and watched every one being very busy. Mummy was cutting bread, Deborah was putting some flowers in a vase of water, and Daddy was looking for a newspaper that had something in it that he specially wanted to read.

Teddy Robinson wished he could look busy too, but he couldn't think of anything to be looking busy about. He stared up at the ceiling. One or two flies were crawling about up there. Teddy Robinson began counting them; but every time he got as far as 'Three' one of them would suddenly fly away and land somewhere quite different, so it was difficult to know if he had counted it before or not.

'What's the matter, Teddy Robinson?' said Deborah.

'Nothing's the matter,' he said. 'I'm busy. I'm counting flies, but they keep flying away.'

'Silly boy,' said Deborah.

'No,' said Mummy, 'he's not silly at all. He's reminded me that I must get some fly-papers from the grocer to-day. We don't want flies crawling about in the kitchen.'

Teddy Robinson felt rather pleased.

'I like being busy,' he said. 'What else can I do?'

Deborah put the vase of flowers on the table beside him.

'You can smell these flowers for me,' she said.

Teddy Robinson leaned forward with his nose against the flowers and smelled them.

When Daddy had found his newspaper and gone off to work, Mummy put some slices of bread under the grill on the cooker.

'We will have some toast,' she said.

'And you can watch it, Teddy Robinson,' said Deborah.

Just then the front-door bell rang, and Mummy went out to see who it was. Teddy Robinson and Deborah could hear Andrew's voice. He was saying something about a picnic this afternoon, and could Deborah come too?

'Oh!' said Deborah. 'I must go and find out about this!' And she ran out into the hall.

Teddy Robinson stayed sitting on the kitchen-table watching the toast. He could hear the others talking by the front door, and then he heard Mummy saying, 'I think I'd better come over and talk to your mummy about it now.' And after that everything was quiet.

Teddy Robinson felt very happy to be so busy. He stared hard at the toast and sang to himself as he watched it turning from

~ watching the toast.

white to golden brown and then from golden brown to black.

In a minute he heard a little snuffling noise coming from the half-open back door. The Puppy from over the Road was peeping into the kitchen. When he saw Teddy Robinson sitting on the table he wagged his tail and smiled, with his pink tongue hanging out.

'What's cooking?' he said.

'Toast,' said Teddy Robinson. 'Won't you come in? There's nobody at home but me.'

'Oh, no, I mustn't,' said the puppy. 'I'm not house-trained yet. Are you?'

'Oh, yes,' said Teddy Robinson. 'I can do quite a lot of useful things in the house.'

He began thinking quickly of all the useful things he could do; then he said, 'I can watch toast, keep people company, smell flowers, time eggs, count flies, or sit on things to keep them from blowing away. Just at the minute I'm watching the toast.'

'It makes an interesting smell, doesn't it?' said the puppy, sniffing the air.

'Yes,' said Teddy Robinson. 'It makes a lot of smoke too. That's what makes it so difficult to watch. You can't see the toast for the smoke, but I've managed to keep my eye on it nearly all the time. I've been making up a little song about it:

'I'm watching the toast.
I don't want to boast,
but I'm better than most
at watching the toast.

'It can bake, it can boil,
it can smoke, it can roast,
but I stick to my post.
I'm watching the toast.'

'Jolly good song,' said the puppy. 'But, you know, it's really awfully smoky in here. If you don't mind I think I'll just go and practise barking at a cat or two until you've finished. Are you sure you won't come out too? Come and have a breath of fresh air.'

'No, no,' said Teddy Robinson. 'I'll stick to my post until the others come back.'

And at that moment the others did come back.

'Oh, dear!' cried Mummy. 'Whatever's happened? Oh, of course – it's the toast! I'd forgotten all about it.'

'But I didn't,' said Teddy Robinson proudly. 'I've been watching it all the time.'

'It was because Andrew came and asked us to a picnic this afternoon,' said Deborah. 'Would you like to come too?'

'I'd much rather stay at home and keep house,' said Teddy Robinson. 'I like being busy. Isn't there something I could do that would be useful?'

'Yes,' said Mummy, when Deborah asked her. 'The grocery order is coming this afternoon. If Teddy Robinson likes to stay he can look after it for us until we come home. We'll ask the man to leave it on the step and risk it.'

So it was decided that Deborah and Mummy should go to the picnic and Teddy Robinson should stay at home and keep house.

When they were all ready to go, Mummy wrote a notice which said, PLEASE LEAVE GROCERIES ON THE STEP, and Deborah wrote underneath it, TEDDY ROBINSON WILL LOOK AFTER THEM. Then they put the notice on the back-door step, and Teddy Robinson sat on it so that it wouldn't blow away.

Deborah kissed him good-bye, and Mummy shut the back door behind him. Teddy Robinson felt very pleased and important, and thought how jolly it was to be so busy that he hadn't even time to go to a picnic.

'I don't care *how* many people come and ask me to picnics or parties to-day,' he said to himself. 'I just can't go to any of them. I'm far too busy.'

Nobody did come to ask Teddy Robinson to a party or a picnic, so after a while he settled down to have a nice, quiet think. His think was all about how lovely it would be if he had a little house all of his own, where he could be as busy as he liked. He had a picture in his mind of how he would open the door to the milkman, and ask the baker to

He had a picture in his mind of how he would open the door to the milkman.

leave one small brown, and invite people in for cups of tea. And he would leave his Wellington boots just outside the door (so as not to make the house muddy), and then say to people, 'Excuse my boots, won't you?' So everybody would notice them, but nobody would think he was showing off about them. (Teddy Robinson hadn't got any Wellington boots, but he was always thinking how nice it would be if he had.)

He began singing to himself in a dreamy sort of way:

'Good morning, baker. One small brown.
How much is that to pay?
Good morning, milkman. Just one pint,
and how's your horse to-day?

'Good afternoon. How nice of you
to come and visit me.
Step right inside (excuse my boots).
I'll make a pot of tea.'

A blackbird flew down and perched on the garden fence. He whistled once or twice, looked at Teddy Robinson with his head on one side, and then flew away again.

A minute later the grocer's boy opened the side gate and came up to the back door. He had a great big cardboard box in his arms.

When he had read the notice he put the big box on the step. Then he picked Teddy Robinson up and sat him on top of it. He grinned at him, then he walked off, whistling loudly and banging the side gate behind him.

The blackbird flew down on to the fence again.

'Was that you whistling?' he asked.

'No,' said Teddy Robinson, 'it was the grocer's boy.'

'Did you hear me whistle just now?' asked the blackbird.

'Yes,' said Teddy Robinson.

'I did it to see if you were real or not,' said the blackbird. 'You were sitting so still I thought you couldn't be, so I whistled to find out. Why didn't you answer me?'

'I can't whistle,' said Teddy Robinson, 'and, anyway, I was thinking.'

'What's in that box?' asked the blackbird. 'Any breadcrumbs?'

Just then there was a scrambling, scuffling noise, and the Puppy from over the Road came lolloping round the corner. The blackbird flew away.

'Hallo,' said the puppy. 'What are you doing here?'

'I'm guarding the groceries,' said Teddy Robinson.

'Well, I never!' said the puppy. 'You were making toast last time I saw you. You do work hard. Do you have to make beds as well?'

'No,' said Teddy Robinson, 'I couldn't make beds. I haven't got a hammer and nails. But I am very busy today.'

'Why don't they take the groceries in?' asked the puppy.

'They've gone to a picnic,' said Teddy Robinson. 'I stayed behind to keep house. They decided to let the boy leave the groceries on the step and risk it.'

'What's "risk-it"?' said the puppy.

'I don't know,' said Teddy Robinson, 'but I like saying it, because it goes so nicely with biscuit.'

'Got any biscuits in there?' asked the puppy, sniffing round the box.

'I'm not sure,' said Teddy Robinson, 'but you mustn't put your nose in the box.'

'I was only sniffing,' said the puppy.

'You mustn't sniff either,' said Teddy Robinson. 'It's a bad habit.'

'What's habit?' said the puppy.

'I don't know,' said Teddy Robinson. 'But it goes very nicely with rabbit.'

Suddenly the back door opened behind him. The puppy scuttled away, and Teddy Robinson found that Deborah and Mummy had come home again.

'You did keep house well,' said Mummy, as she carried him into the kitchen with the box of groceries.

'Don't you think he ought to have a present,' said Deborah, 'for being so good at housekeeping?'

'He really ought to have a house of his own,' said Mummy. 'Look – what about this?' She pointed to the big box. 'You could make him a nice house out of that when it's empty. I'll help you to cut the windows out.'

'Oh, *yes*,' said Deborah, 'that is exactly what he wants.'

So after tea Deborah and Mummy got busy making a beautiful little house for Teddy Robinson. They made a door and two windows (one at the front and one at the back) and painted them green. Then Deborah made a hole in the lid of the box and stuck a cardboard chimney in it. Mummy painted a rambler-rose climbing up the wall. It looked very pretty.

'What would you like to call your house?' said Deborah. 'Do you think Rose Cottage would be a nice name?'

'I'd rather it had my own name on it,' said Teddy Robinson.

So Deborah painted TEDDY ROBINSON'S HOUSE over the door, and then it was all ready.

The next day Teddy Robinson's house was put out in the garden in the sunshine. He chose to have it close to the flower-bed at the edge of the lawn, and all day long he sat inside and waited for people to call on him. Deborah came to see him quite often, and every time she looked in at the window and said, 'What are you doing now, Teddy Robinson?' he would say, 'I'm just thinking about what to have for dinner,' or 'I'm just having a rest before getting tea.'

The Puppy from over the Road came and called on him too. He sniffed at Teddy Robinson through the

open window and admired him more than ever now that he had a house of his own.

And the garden tortoise came tramping out of the flower-bed and looked up at the house, saying, 'Well, well, I never knew there was a house there!'

"I never knew there was a house there"

Then the next-door kitten came walking round on tiptoe. At first she didn't quite believe it was real. She was sniffing at the rambler-rose painted on the wall when Teddy Robinson looked out of the window and said, 'Good afternoon.'

The kitten purred with pleasure at seeing him.

'What a purr-r-rfect little house!' she said. 'Is it really yours? You *are* a lucky purr-r-rson.'

Teddy Robinson nodded and smiled at her from the window.

'Yes,' he said, 'it's my very own house. Aren't I lucky? It's just what I've always wanted – a little place all of my own.'

And that is the end of the story about how Teddy Robinson kept house.

The cormorant and the bears

ANON

The common cormorant or shag
Lays eggs inside a paper bag.
The reason you will see no doubt:
It is to keep the lightning out.
But what these unobservant birds
Have never noticed is that herds
Of wandering bears may come with buns
And steal the bags to hold the crumbs.